MIRACLES IN ORDINARY MOMENTS

"Discovering Divine Grace in Everyday Life"

BY AUTHOR: LIONEL B. PEARSON

MIRACLES in ORDINARY MOMENTS

"Discovering Divine Grace in Everyday Life"

LIONEL B. PEARSON

Copyright © Lionel B. Pearson 2023

All rights reserved. No part of this publication may be reproduced, distributed, or transmitted in any form or by any means, including

photocopying, recording, or other electronic or mechanical methods, without the prior written permission of the publisher, except in the case of brief quotations embodied in critical reviews and certain other noncommercial uses permitted by copyright law.

This is a work of fiction. Names, characters, places, and incidents either are the product of the author's imagination or are used fictitiously. Any resemblance to actual persons, living or dead, events, or locales is entirely coincidental.

eBook ISBN 978-1-7373575-2-0

Paperback ISBN: 978-1-7373575-3-7

Published by D'Tor Publishing

837 Lyndhurst St., Balto., Md., 21229

For inquiries, please contact:

Pastor Lionel B. Pearson (443) 461-4100

DEDICATION PAGE

"To God, the source of all Inspiration and Grace. This book is dedicated to His divine presence, which has guided every word and every thought on these pages."

TABLE OF CONTENTS

Chapter 1 1

Chapter 2 4

Chapter 3 7

Chapter 4 13

Chapter 5 16

Chapter 6 19

Chapter 7 22

Chapter 8 26

Chapter 9 32

Chapter 10 35

Chapter 11 39

Chapter 12 42

Chapter 13 46

Chapter 14 49

Chapter 15 52

Acknowledgments 55

Part 1: Threads of Discovery

CHAPTER 1

A Glimpse of Grace

The sun dipped toward the horizon, casting a warm, golden glow over the quiet suburban street. Sarah's steps were purposeful, each one a beat in the rhythm of her thoughts. The challenges of her career had left her drained, and personal struggles had cast a shadow over her usual optimism. Lost in her internal monologue, she barely noticed the elderly woman kneeling in her garden up ahead.

Mrs. Thompson, her neighbor, was a fixture of the community. With her silver hair and peaceful smile, she had an air of wisdom that drew people to her. Today, she was tending to her flowers with meticulous care, as if each bloom held a secret she alone could understand.

As Sarah approached, Mrs. Thompson looked up, her gaze locking onto Sarah's with an uncanny precision. Her eyes crinkled in a friendly smile.

"Good evening, dear."

Caught off guard, Sarah blinked and then offered a polite smile. "Good evening, Mrs. Thompson."

The older woman straightened up; her gardening gloves dusted with soil.

"Beautiful sunset, isn't it? A reminder of God's imagination."

Sarah's glance flickered toward the sky, sorts of orange and yellow painting the heavens. It was indeed a sight to behold, but her mind was too preoccupied to fully appreciate it. "Yes, it is," she replied, her voice distant.

Mrs. Thompson's eyes seemed to penetrate beyond the surface. "You seem troubled, my dear. A heavy heart doesn't go unnoticed."

Sarah's eyebrows crumpled. "It's just... work and life, you know?"

The older woman nodded knowingly. "Ah, yes. The weight of responsibilities and challenges. But in those moments, it's important to remember that grace can be found even in the ordinary."

Sarah's curiosity was piqued, her thoughts momentarily diverted. "Grace? In ordinary moments?"

Mrs. Thompson's smile held a quiet wisdom. "Especially in ordinary moments. You see, dear, God's grace isn't confined to grand events. It's in the quiet moments, the everyday occurrences that we sometimes overlook."

Sarah's skepticism gave way to genuine interest. "You really believe that?"

"Absolutely," Mrs. Thompson affirmed. "In the laughter of children, the kindness of strangers, the whisper of the wind—those are all moments where we catch a glimpse of God's grace."

Sarah felt a hint of her defenses crumbling, replaced by a longing to understand. "So, you're saying that even in the midst of challenges, there's grace?"

Mrs. Thompson's gaze was steady. "Especially in the midst of challenges. It's during those times that we often see grace most clearly, like a light shining in the darkness."

As Sarah listened, a warmth began to spread within her. She realized that she had been so caught up in her own worries that she had missed the small moments of beauty and grace that surrounded her.

With a gentle nod, Mrs. Thompson returned to her gardening, her fingers expertly tending to the delicate petals. "I've learned over the years that life is a series of moments, each one holding the potential to reveal God's presence."

Sarah found herself drawn to Mrs. Thompson's presence, her words like a soothing balm for her weary soul. "And you think grace is in all those moments?"

Mrs. Thompson turned back to Sarah, her eyes shining with conviction. "Yes, Sarah. Yes. Every sunrise, every act of kindness, every unexpected joy—those are all music notes of grace in the chords of our lives."

Sarah felt a lump forming in her throat, her emotions swirling within her.

"Thank you, Mrs. Thompson. I really needed to hear that."

The elderly woman's gaze was gentle. "Anytime, Sarah, anytime. Just remember, grace is never far away. It's tied up, and tangled up into every moment, waiting to be recognized."

As Sarah continued her walk, the weight that had been pressing on her heart seemed to lighten just a bit. She looked up at the sky once more, the vivid colors taking on a new significance. A sense of gratitude began to well up within her, and for the first time in a while, she felt a glimmer of hope.

When she stepped into her house, Sarah couldn't shake the feeling that this encounter was something special. Mrs. Thompson's words had touched her deeply, reminding her to see beyond her worries and challenges. Perhaps there was indeed grace waiting to be found in the ordinary moments she had been overlooking.

As she prepared for bed that night, Sarah whispered a prayer of gratitude for a peek of grace she had received. Little did she know that this encounter would mark the beginning of a journey—a journey to discover the extraordinary in the ordinary moments of life.

CHAPTER 2

The Whispering Breeze

Ethan had always been captivated by the world around him—the intricate details of a flower's petals, the interplay of light and shadow, the everchanging colors of the sky. As an artist, he saw beauty in places others might overlook, and he sought to capture these moments on his canvas.

Yet, beneath the surface of his artistic pursuits, Ethan grappled with his own internal struggles. The recent loss of his beloved grandmother had left a void in his heart, and he found himself questioning the meaning of life and the existence of a higher purpose.

One crisp morning, Ethan took his easel and paints to the nearby park, hoping to find inspiration in the tranquility of nature. He set up his canvas overlooking a pond, where the water shimmered like liquid glass under the early morning sun. Birds chirped in the distance, their melodies harmonizing with the rustling leaves.

As Ethan dipped his brush into the palette, he felt a sense of frustration. The colors seemed dull, and his strokes lacked the usual zeal. He gazed at the blank canvas, willing his emotions to translate onto the surface, but it was as if his creativity had deserted him.

In the midst of his frustration, a gentle breeze stirred, ruffling the pages of his notebook and sending a shiver down his spine. He looked up; his eyes were spread wide open as he witnessed the dance of leaves on the trees.

The breeze seemed to whisper secrets to the world, as if it carried a message meant only for those who were willing to listen.

Ethan's gaze shifted to the pond, where ripples spread across the water's surface in response to the breeze's touch. It was as if the breeze was orchestrating a symphony with nature itself—a complex composition of movement, sound, and color.

As he watched, an idea began to take shape within Ethan's mind. He dipped his brush into the blue paint, mixing it with a touch of white to capture the refined quality of the breeze. With each stroke, he sought to convey the way the breeze stirred the trees, creating a rhythm that echoed in the heartbeats of all living things.

Time seemed to blur as Ethan lost himself in his work. The frustration that had weighed him down earlier had transformed into a sense of purpose, a determination to capture the mysterious beauty that had always been present in the world around him.

As he painted, he began to reflect on the concept of grace—the idea that even during uncertainty and loss, there was a guiding force that breathed life into every moment. He recalled stories from his grandmother, who had always spoken of God's presence in creation, in the whispers of the wind and the songs of the birds.

With each brushstroke, Ethan sought to bring life to the idea of the whispering breeze—an unseen presence that moved through life's challenges and triumphs, carrying with it a message of hope and renewal. The canvas began to come alive, the colors blending seamlessly to create an image that seemed to shimmer and sway with the breeze's rhythm.

As the sun climbed higher in the sky, Ethan stepped back from his canvas, his heart racing with a mixture of exhaustion and exhilaration. He gazed at the painting, his eyes tracing the lines and curves that captured the essence of the breeze.

And then, something remarkable happened. A soft swishing of leaves sounded behind him, and he turned to see a group of children standing there, their eyes wide with wonder as they looked at his painting. One of the children, a young girl with ponytails, turned to him with a smile.

"It's like the trees are dancing," she said, her voice filled with awe.

Ethan smiled back, his heart swelling with gratitude. "Yes, exactly. It's the whispering breeze that makes them dance."

The children gathered around the painting, their fingers reaching out as if to touch the breeze itself. In that moment, in that very moment Ethan realized that his work had transcended the canvas—it had become a bridge, connecting him to the world and those who saw his creation.

As the children continued to admire the painting, Ethan closed his eyes and felt the breeze on his skin, as if it were a gentle embrace from his grandmother's spirit. He understood that he was part of something greater—a symphony of life, a dance of creation that was guided by a divine hand.

And so, as the children's laughter echoed in the park, Ethan knew that he had found the inspiration he had been searching for. He had discovered that the whispering breeze was not just a force of nature—it was a reminder that beauty, meaning, and grace could be found in every moment, if only one had the eyes to see and the heart to listen.

CHAPTER 3

Threads of Connection

The sun hung low in the sky, casting a warm golden glow over the town's paved streets. Michael had a relax stroll to his walk, his hands shoved into the pockets of his jacket, lost in thought. He had moved to this quiet town seeking comfort from the dreaded sound of his past, and today, with the gentle breeze carrying the scent of freshly baked bread, he felt a flicker of hope in his heart.

As he walked past this attractive bakery, the aroma of cinnamon and vanilla traveled through the air, drawing his attention to a woman sitting on a nearby bench. Her hazel eyes were locked onto the pages of a book, her fingers delicately turning each page as if she were treasuring every word.

Curiosity got the best of him, and with a hesitant smile, he approached her. "Is that a good read?" he asked, his voice carrying a hint of vulnerability he hadn't intended.

Startled, the woman looked up, her lips parting in surprise before breaking into a warm smile. "Oh, yes, quite captivating. It's a story about faith and redemption. I've found it quite inspiring."

Michael's interest deepened, and he couldn't help but be drawn in by the sparkle in her eyes. "I could use some inspiration myself these days."

Rachel closed the book, her fingers marking the page she'd been reading.

"Don't we all," she replied, her tone carrying a touch of empathy. "I'm

Rachel, by the way."

"Michael," he said, offering a hand, which she shook with a firm yet gentle grip. He noticed the hint of a scar on her palm, a detail that spoke of a story he was eager to learn.

They began to talk, and the initial awkwardness gave way to a natural flow of conversation. Rachel shared about her journey to this town, her reasons for moving, and the desire to be closer to her grandparents, who had been her rock since childhood.

Michael found himself opening up about his own experiences—the pain of a recent divorce, the pieces of himself he felt he had lost in the process. The more he spoke, the more he realized that Rachel was listening not just with her ears, but with her heart.

Rachel leaned in; her eyes filled with compassion. "You know, Michael, sometimes it's the challenges that shape us into who we're meant to be."

He looked at her, a mixture of surprise and gratitude in his eyes. "You really believe that?"

She nodded, her expression earnest. "Absolutely. It's like the story of Ruth and Naomi. They faced tremendous difficulties, but through their loyalty and love for each other, they found strength and purpose."

Their conversation flowed freely, and as the sun dipped below the horizon, they found themselves still talking, as if the passage of time had ceased to matter. The topics shifted from books to life's mysteries, and somewhere along the way, Michael felt a warmth in his chest that he hadn't experienced in a long time.

As the evening ended, Rachel closed her book, her fingers lingering on the pages as if reluctant to part with the world it held. "Would you like to continue this conversation over a cup of coffee?" Michael asked, surprising himself with the invitation.

Her smile was genuine, and her eyes held a spark of curiosity. "I'd like that," she replied.

The café was cozy, with the aroma of freshly brewed coffee mingling with the faint sound of soft jazz playing in the background. Michael and Rachel sat across from each other, their cups steaming as they shared stories of their lives.

Rachel's voice was animated as she recounted tales of her grandparent's wisdom, painting a vivid picture of a woman whose strength had weathered the storms of time. "My grandparents took turns telling me that even in the midst of chaos, God's presence is like a thread that weaves through every moment, connecting us to something greater."

Michael leaned in, captivated by her words. "Threads of connection," he murmured, the phrase ringing within him.

Rachel nodded, her eyes locking onto his. "Exactly. We may not always see the whole picture, but when we look back, we can see how each thread was necessary to create something beautiful."

The hours slipped by unnoticed, and as they parted ways, Michael felt a sense of anticipation he hadn't felt in years. As he lay in bed that night, he reflected on the stories Rachel had shared—the stories that had tugged at his heartstrings, reminding him that he was not alone in his struggles.

In the days that followed, Michael and Rachel's interactions became a regular occurrence. They attended a local Bible study together, where they dug deeper into the story of Ruth and Naomi. The parallels between their lives and the lives of these biblical women became more apparent, and as they discussed the themes of loyalty, love, and finding family in unexpected places, Michael felt a newfound sense of purpose.

With each passing day, the threads of connection between them grew stronger. Just as Ruth had remained steadfast by Naomi's side, Rachel was a constant source of encouragement and companionship for Michael. He found himself looking forward to their conversations, eager to learn from her insights and wisdom.

As they spent time together, Michael discovered that Rachel had a scar on her palm—a result of a childhood accident. She shared how that scar was a reminder of the challenges she had overcome and the strength she had gained through them. It was a tangible representation of the threads of connection that intertwined through her own story.

With Rachel's guidance, Michael began to see his own scars—the emotional wounds left by his divorce—in a new light. He realized that they, too, were threads that contributed to the tapestry of his life, shaping him into the person he was becoming.

As the seasons changed, so did their relationship. The warmth of summer gave way to the vibrant colors of autumn, and Michael found himself falling in love with Rachel's compassionate spirit. Her ability to see beauty in every moment, to find hope even in the face of adversity, was a quality he admired deeply.

Rachel, too, discovered a connection that went beyond mere friendship. As they shared their stories, they realized that their meeting was not a random occurrence, but a thread woven into the fabric of God's plan. Their paths had crossed at a time when they both needed a glimmer of hope, a reminder that even in the midst of challenges, there was beauty waiting to be discovered.

And so, their story became a testament to the threads of connection that God weaves into our lives. Each moment, each encounter, was a thread that added depth and richness to the textile of their journey. Through Rachel's influence, Michael learned to see his own life with new eyes, recognizing the significance of the scars he carried and the potential for growth and transformation.

As autumn faded into winter, their bond continued to grow stronger. With each passing day, they discovered new layers of their shared story, finding comfort in the fact that they were not alone in their struggles. The story of Ruth and Naomi served as a constant reminder that even in the darkest of times, there was always a glimmer of light, a thread of hope, waiting to be discovered.

And so, as they navigated life's twists and turns together, Michael and Rachel held onto the threads of connection that had brought them together. They learned to see the beauty in the tapestry of their lives, recognizing that every moment, every challenge, and every triumph was a part of a larger design. It was a design that laced their individual stories into a greater narrative—one that spoke of faith, redemption, and the unbreakable bonds that could be formed through love and friendship.

One brisk winter morning, as snowflakes gently fell from the sky, Michael found himself standing outside Rachel's door, a bouquet of freshly picked flowers in hand. He had come to realize that the connection they shared was something truly special, and he wanted to express his feelings in a way that went beyond words.

As Rachel opened the door, her eyes widened in surprise at the sight of Michael standing there, a nervous yet hopeful smile on his face. "Michael, what a wonderful surprise!" she yelled, her cheeks flushed from the cold.

He extended the bouquet towards her, his heart racing. "These are for you," he said simply.

Rachel accepted the flowers with a radiant smile, her eyes sparkling with gratitude. "Thank you, Michael. They're beautiful."

As they stood in the doorway, a sense of anticipation hung in the air. Michael took a deep breath, gathering his courage. "Rachel, I've come to realize that the threads of connection between us are stronger than I ever imagined. You've brought so much light into my life, and I want to be a part of yours as well."

Rachel's smile grew even wider, and her eyes held a mixture of joy and understanding. "Michael, I feel the same way. The moments we've shared, the conversations we've had—they've shown me the beauty of finding a kindred spirit."

He took a step closer, his gaze locked onto hers. "Would you do me the honor of allowing me to be a part of your story?"

Her response was a heartfelt embrace, one that spoke volumes without the need for words. In that clinch, they both felt the warmth of a connection that had blossomed against all odds, a connection that had been merged into their lives by a divine hand.

As they pulled away from the embrace, their eyes met once again, and Michael knew that this was a moment he would treasure forever. "Rachel," he said softly, "this feels like a thread of connection that's meant to last a lifetime."

She nodded, her eyes misting with emotion. "I believe that too, Michael. Just like Ruth and Naomi, we've found strength and purpose in each other's company."

And in that moment, as the snow continued to fall around them, Michael and Rachel embraced the threads of connection that had brought them together.

They realized that their individual stories, with all their challenges and triumphs, had led them to this point—a point where they were ready to board on a new chapter of their lives, hand in hand.

Their story would continue to unfold, guided by the threads of connection they had discovered in the ordinary moments of life. And as they faced the future together, they held onto the knowledge that every thread, every moment, was a part of God's elaborate design—a design that had brought two souls together to create a tapestry of love, faith, and shared purpose.

CHAPTER 4

Seeds of Hope

The morning sun cast a warm glow over the small garden that Lachelle tended with care. Each blossom seemed to nod in gratitude, as if acknowledging her efforts to nurture and protect them. Among the vibrant colors and delicate petals, Lachelle found comfort—a quiet refuge from the challenges that life had thrown her way.

As a single mother, Lachelle's days were a delicate balancing act, filled with the demands of work, parenting, and the constant struggle to make ends meet. The recent loss of her job had intensified the weight on her shoulders, leaving her feeling overwhelmed and uncertain about the future.

One evening, as Lachelle sat at the kitchen table, poring over job listings with a wrinkled brow, her young daughter, Jazmine, approached with a drawing in hand. With a hopeful smile, Jazmine presented her masterpiece— a simple description of a tiny seed surrounded by soil.

"Mommy, I drew this for you," Jazmine said, her eyes shining with excitement.

Lachelle looked down at the drawing, her heart melting at the sight of her daughter's innocent creation. "It's beautiful, sweetheart. What's it about?"

Jazmine's eyes sparkled as she explained, "It's like the seed is small, but it's gonna grow into something big and strong. Just like us!"

Lachelle felt a lump forming in her throat as she looked at her daughter's drawing. In those words, Jazmine had unknowingly captured the essence of their situation—a small seed of hope while in the middle of adversity.

That night, as Lachelle tucked Jazmine into bed, she lingered for a moment, watching her daughter's peaceful expression. Jazmine's words echoed in her mind, and a spark of inspiration ignited within her. She realized that even during challenges, there was strength to be found in the smallest glimmers of hope.

The following morning, Lachelle woke up with renewed determination. She put on her gardening gloves and headed out to the garden, her heart set on a task she hadn't attempted before. With a packet of seeds in hand, she began to carefully prepare the soil, her fingers working with a sense of purpose.

As the seeds were gently placed into the earth, Lachelle couldn't help but draw parallels between these tiny seeds and the dreams she held for her family. She thought about how faith was often described as small as a mustard seed, yet it had the power to move mountains. With each seed she planted, she was planting a seed of hope—a tangible reminder that even the smallest acts of faith could yield remarkable results.

Days turned into weeks, and Lachelle tended to her garden with unwavering dedication. She watered the soil, protected the fragile shoots, and watched as new life emerged from the earth. The garden became a testament to her resilience, a symbol of her belief that even in the face of adversity, there was potential for growth and beauty.

One afternoon, as Lachelle was tending to the garden, a knock at the door caught her attention. She wiped her hands on her apron and opened the door to find her neighbor, Mr. Jefferson, standing there with a warm smile.

"Hey, Lachelle. I've been watching you work on that garden of yours," he said, his eyes crinkling with kindness.

Lachelle returned the smile, feeling a sense of friendship. "It's been helping me through some tough times."

Mr. Jefferson nodded, his gaze moving to the vibrant flowers that now beautified the once barren ground. "You know, sometimes it's the small things that hold the most promise. Just like those seeds you planted." Lachelle's heart warmed at his words, realizing that he understood the significance of her efforts. "Thank you, Mr. Jefferson."

He tipped his hat and turned to leave, but then he paused and looked back at Lachelle. "You know, Lachelle, you remind me of a story I once heard. It's about a mustard seed—small but full of potential."

Lachelle's eyes widened as she listened, captivated by Mr. Jefferson's story. It was as if his words were a confirmation of her own journey, a reminder that even when life felt challenging and uncertain, there was a strength within her that could thrive.

As the weeks went by, Lachelle's garden continued to show promise, its beauty a testament to her unwavering faith and determination. And just as Jazmine had imagined, the small seeds had indeed grown into something big and strong—a reflection of the resilience and hope that Lachelle carried within her heart.

Lachelle knew that life's challenges would continue to come her way, but she had discovered a truth that would guide her through every storm: the power of a seed of hope, planted with faith and nurtured with love, could transform even the most barren of landscapes into a garden of possibility.

CHAPTER 5

The Unseen Hand

The ancient oak tree stood tall and grand, its branches reaching upward as if in silent praise. Jerome leaned against the tree, his thoughts spin of memories and questions. The events of the past year had left him wrestling with doubt, his once unshakable faith now trembling in the face of adversity.

As he stared at the complex patterns of sunlight streaming through the leaves, Jerome's mind began to wander about the story of Abraham. He remembered how Abraham had been called to sacrifice his son, Isaac—a test of faith that had ultimately revealed God's providence and mercy.

Jerome's own journey had been marked by challenges that had tested his faith in ways he had never imagined. The loss of his job, the strain on his relationships, and the unexpected health issues—all of it had left him feeling lost, torn, and broken, as if the threads of his life had unraveled.

He closed his eyes, his fingers tracing the rough bark of the oak tree. Bending his head slightly toward heaven Jerome whispered, "God, if you're there, if you are listening, if you're guiding my footsteps, then please show me a sign. Let me see your unseen hand working on behave."

The wind rustled through the leaves, and Jerome took it as a gentle reply. With a breath, he opened his eyes, his eyes drawn to a single leaf that detached from a branch and slowly fell to the ground. It was a simple sight, yet it held a quiet beauty that captured his attention.

As he watched the leaf settle on the ground, he realized that even in the seemingly routine, there was evidence of an unseen hand at work—a complex design that governed the world's rhythms and cycles. And just as the leaf had fallen in its perfect time, so too did the events of life unfold according to a divine plan.

As Jerome contemplated these thoughts, a voice broke through his daydream. "Beautiful, isn't it?"

Startled, Jerome turned to find an elderly man standing nearby, a warm smile on his face. His eyes held a depth of wisdom that seemed to reach into Jerome's very soul.

"I'm sorry, I didn't mean to intrude," the man said, his voice gentle. "I couldn't help but notice your contemplation."

Jerome shook his head, feeling a sense of friendship in the stranger's presence. "No, you're not intruding. It's just... I've been wrestling with my faith, and I find myself questioning the purpose behind everything."

The man nodded; his gaze thoughtful. "Life has a way of leading us to those moments of questioning. But sometimes, the answers come when we least expect them."

Jerome's curiosity was piqued. "Do you believe that everything happens for a reason?"

The man smiled, his eyes reflecting a depth of understanding. "I believe that God's hand is always at work, even when we can't see it. Just like the leaf falling from the tree—you can't always predict when or why, but there's a purpose in its journey."

As Jerome listened, he felt a sense of meaning with the man's words. It was as if the stranger was echoing the very thoughts that had been spinning within him.

"Abraham," the man continued, "had to trust in the unseen hand of God, even when the path seemed unclear. And in the end, he discovered that the challenges he faced were part of a greater plan—one that led to redemption and renewal."

Tears formed up in Jerome's eyes as he gripped on to the stranger's words. It was as if his doubts were being addressed, his questions met with a reassurance that he hadn't anticipated.

"I've been struggling to find that trust," Jerome stated, his voice barely above a whisper.

The man's smile was kind, his presence an inspiration of relief. "It's okay to doubt. It's a part of the journey. But remember, sometimes all it takes is a shift in perspective—a recognition that the unseen hand of God is orchestrating something beautiful, even during challenges."

As the stranger walked away, leaving Jerome with his thoughts, a sense of calm settled over him. He looked up at the oak tree, its branches swaying gently in the wind, and he realized that he didn't need all the answers. He didn't need to see every step of the journey laid out before him.

With renewed faith, Jerome understood that the challenges he faced were not without purpose. Just as the leaf fell to the ground in perfect timing, so too did the events of his life unfold according to a divine plan—an unseen hand guiding him, even when he couldn't fully comprehend the path.

And as he leaned against the age-old oak, Jerome felt a sense of peace—a quiet assurance that the challenges he faced were not impossible, and that the unseen hand of God was leading him to redemption and renewal, just as it had done for Abraham.

Part 2 Dancing in Raindrops

CHAPTER 6

Dancing in Raindrops

The sound of rain tapping against the window filled the air as Lynette watched the raindrops race each other down the glass pane. It was a rainy afternoon, and Lynette and Estelle had decided to spend the day indoors, seeking refuge from the downpour outside.

"Mommy, why does it rain?" Estelle asked, her curious eyes fixed on the world outside.

Lynette smiled, glad for the opportunity to share a moment of learning with her daughter. "Rain happens when the clouds get full of water. Then, the water falls from the clouds, and that's what we call rain."

Estelle's watch never shook from the window, her mind clearly processing the information. "So, the clouds are like big water tanks?"

Lynette chuckled softly. "Yes, something like that."

As the rain continued to fall, Lynette's thoughts turned to the simple joys that rainy days had brought into their lives. She remembered how, when Estelle was younger, they used to dance in the rain together. It was a tradition they had started—one that had brought laughter, joy, and a sense of freedom.

With a spark of inspiration, Lynette turned to Estelle. "You know what, sweetheart? How about we dance in the rain today?"

Estelle's eyes lit up with excitement. "Really, Mommy? Even though we're inside?"

Lynette nodded, her heartwarming at her daughter's zeal. "Yes, really. We might not get wet, but we can still dance and have fun."

With eager anticipation, Lynette and Estelle moved to the center of the living room. Lynette opened the window slightly, allowing the faint scent of rain to blow into the room. They held hands, their fingers locked, and began to move to a fantasy rhythm.

The sound of raindrops outside seemed to become a part of their dance, a gentle percussion that accompanied their movements. Lynette twirled Estelle around, and they laughed together, their spirits lifted by the simple act of dancing.

As they danced, Lynette's thoughts turned to the story of King David, who had danced before the Lord with all his might. She imagined that their own unrehearsed dance was a similar expression of gratitude and joy—an offering of their hearts to the beauty of the moment.

After a while, Lynette's phone buzzed with a text message, interrupting their dance. She picked up the phone and read the message, her smile fading as she absorbed its contents. It was news about a job opportunity—an interview that she had been waiting for. As she read the message, a mixture of excitement and nervousness washed over her.

Estelle noticed the change in her mother's expression and tugged on her hand. "What's wrong, Mommy?"

Lynette's look shifted from the phone to Estelle's concerned eyes. She took a deep breath, her fingers still locked with her daughter's. "It's nothing to worry about, sweetheart. Mommy has a job interview, and I'm just feeling a little nervous."

Estelle's brow wrinkled with understanding. "You're always telling me to be brave. Now it's your turn, Mommy."

Lynette felt a lump forming in her throat as she looked at her daughter—the example of courage and hope. Estelle was right. She had always encouraged her daughter to be brave in the face of challenges, and now it was her turn to take her own advice.

With a determined smile, Lynette nodded. "You're right, Estelle. Thank you for reminding me. Let's continue our dance and celebrate the possibilities."

As they returned to their dance, Lynette felt a renewed sense of purpose and confidence. The raindrops outside seemed to dance with them, a reminder that even during life's uncertainties, there was beauty to be found.

And so, as the rain continued to fall and Lynette and Estelle twirled and laughed together, they discovered that their dance was not just a physical expression—it was a celebration of life's moments, a reminder that even in the rainiest of days, there was a reason to dance and find joy.

As the rain gradually subsided, Lynette and Estelle slowed their dance, their breathing a little quicker, their hearts a little lighter. They held each other close, the memory of their dance imprinted on their souls—a testament to the bond they shared and the simple moments that had the power to lighten even the darkest of days.

As Lynette looked into her daughter's eyes, she knew that this rainy-day dance would forever be a cherished memory—a reminder that in life's storms, they could always find reasons to dance, to laugh, and to hold the beauty that could be found in raindrops.

CHAPTER 7

Embracing the Unexpected

The hospital room was bathed in a soft, sterile light as Tiffani lay on the crisp white sheets, her thoughts a wild mix of worry and uncertainty. Tubes and machines surrounded her, their presence a reminder of the brittleness of life. She stared at the ceiling, her mind a whirlwind of questions, her heart heavy with the weight of her situation.

The past few weeks had been a blur—a series of doctor's appointments, tests, and consultations. The diagnosis had come as a shock—a serious health condition that required immediate treatment and an uncertain path ahead.

Tiffani's fingers fiddled with the edge of the blanket as she replayed the doctor's words in her mind. The treatment plan was scary, the prediction uncertain, and the journey ahead filled with challenges she hadn't anticipated.

As if sensing her turmoil, the door to her hospital room creaked open, and her best friend, Monica, entered with a bouquet of vibrant flowers in hand. Monica's eyes held a mixture of concern and compassion as she approached Tiffani's bedside.

"Hey Girl!!," Monica said softly, her voice a comforting presence in the room. "I brought you these. I thought they might brighten up your space a little bit."

Tiffani managed a weak smile as she accepted the flowers, her fingers brushing against the soft petals. "Thank you, Monica. You always know how to bring a little light into the darkness."

Monica took a seat beside Tiffani, her stare never leaving her friend's face.

"How are you holding up Tiff?"

Tiffani's smile faded, and she looked down at her hands. "Honestly, I don't even know anymore. It's all so overwhelming."

Monica reached out and placed a gentle hand on Tiffani's, offering a silent gesture of support. "You don't have to go through this alone, you know that don't you? I'm here for you every step of the way."

Tears welled up in Tiffani's eyes as she met Monica's gaze—a gaze that held a depth of friendship and understanding that words could not express. "I'm scared, Monica. I'm scared of what's ahead, of the unknown."

Monica squeezed Tiffani's hand, her voice steady and reassuring. "It's okay to be scared. But remember, you're not alone in this. We're facing this together, and we'll find the strength to overcome whatever comes our way."

As Tiffani gripped Monica's words, she felt a sense of comfort wash over her—a reminder that even during life's storms, there were anchors of support and love that could steady her.

Days turned into weeks, and Tiffani's hospital room became a familiar haven—a place where conversations with Monica, visits from loved ones, and moments of quiet reflection all tied together to form an ounce of strength.

One evening, as the sun set in a blaze of orange and yellow tones outside the window, Tiffani found herself deep in thought. She remembered the story of Job—a man who had faced unimaginable challenges and yet had found a way to cling to his faith.

Monica, who had been sitting by her side, noticed Tiffani's thoughtful expression. "What's on your mind?"

Tiffani hesitated before speaking, her voice carrying a mixture of vulnerability and determination. "I've been thinking about Job, and how he held onto his faith even during suffering. I want to find that kind of strength—the ability to embrace the unexpected with courage."

Monica nodded, her eyes reflecting Tiffani's ideas. "You already have that strength within you, Tiffani. You've faced challenges with grace and determination."

Tiffani looked out the window at the fading sunlight, a sense of resolve growing within her. "You're right. Maybe this is a chance for me to embrace life in a new way—to find meaning even in the unexpected."

As the days passed, Tiffani's treatment began—a series of procedures and therapies that required both physical and emotional endurance. And through it all, Monica remained by her side, offering steadfast support and a listening ear.

One day, as Tiffani's strength began to return, she decided to take mission walk outside the hospital for the first time in weeks. Monica wheeled her in a wheelchair to a small garden area just beyond the building's entry. The scent of promising flowers filled the air, and the gentle breeze whispered promises of renewal.

Tiffani closed her eyes, her face turned toward the sun's warmth. "I never realized how much I took for granted—the simple pleasures of life."

Monica smiled; her gaze fixed on her friend. "Sometimes, it takes facing challenges to truly appreciate the beauty around us."

Tiffani opened her eyes and met Monica's gaze—a gaze that held a depth of friendship, sisterhood, and shared experiences. "Thank you, Monica. Thank you for being there for me, for reminding me that even in the midst of uncertainty, there is hope."

Monica reached out and gripped Tiffani's hand, their fingers interlocking as a symbol of unity. "I told you girl, you're never alone, Tiff. We're in this journey together, and I believe that even during life's unexpected twists, there is a grace that guides us."

As they sat together in the garden, surrounded by the beauty of nature and the promise of a new day, Tiffani felt a sense of renewal coursing through her veins. She knew that the challenges she faced were not impossible, and that even in the face of the unexpected, she had the support of a friend who was willing to journey alongside her.

And as the sun dipped below the horizon, casting a warm glow across the garden, Tiffani and Monica found relief in the knowledge that their friendship was a beacon of light—a reminder that even during life's storms, there was beauty to be found, grace to be embraced, and the strength to face whatever lay ahead.

CHAPTER 8

Footprints of Faith

The waves crashed against the rocky shoreline, their rhythm a constant reminder of the decline and flow of life's challenges. Sean stood on the edge of the cliff; the salty breeze cools his baldhead from the beams of the shinning sun as he looked out at the vast expanse of the ocean. In his heart, he carried a burden—a weight of regrets and mistakes that seemed to hold him captive.

As an artist, Sean had always found comfort in his work—a way to express his thoughts and emotions through his creations. But lately, a cloud of self-doubt had settled over his artistic attempts, leaving him feeling uninspired and disconnected from the very passion that had once fueled his spirit.

With a sigh, Sean turned away from the ocean and began to go down the rocky path that led down to the beach. His steps were heavy, each one a reminder of the internal struggle he faced. He walked along the shore, lost in his thoughts, his eyes fixed on the sand beneath his feet.

It was then that he noticed something—two sets of footprints imprinted in the sand, side by side. Sean's curiosity was piqued, and he followed the trail of footprints, his eyes widening as he realized that they seemed to lead toward a massive rock formation that extended out into the sea.

As he approached the rock, he noticed a small tablet at its base. Curious, he leaned closer to read the inscription: "Walk by faith, not by sight."

The words struck a chord within Sean —a reminder that even when life's path seemed uncertain, there was a guiding force that could be trusted. He looked out at the ocean once more, its extent a reflection of the unknown journey that lay ahead.

With a renewed sense of purpose, Sean returned to his art studio. He picked up his paintbrush and began to work, allowing his emotions to flow onto the canvas. Each stroke of the brush seemed to carry a piece of his heart, his doubts and fears transformed into bright shades and intricate patterns.

Days turned into weeks, and Sean's studio became a sanctuary—a place where he wrestled with his doubts, wrestled with his mistakes, and found relief in the act of creation. He painted a series of pieces, each one a testament to his journey of faith and self-discovery.

One evening, as Sean put the finishing touches on a particularly difficult painting, he noticed a visitor standing in the doorway—a young girl with a backpack slung over her shoulder. Her eyes held a mixture of curiosity and awe as they moved over the paintings that beautified the walls.

"Hello," Sean said with a smile, his heart warming at the sight of the young girl.

The girl approached the painting that Sean had just finished, her eyes fixed on the vibrant colors and sophisticated patterns. "Wow, these are amazing. Did you paint them?"

Sean nodded, his eyes meeting the girl's. "Yes, I did. I'm an artist."

The girl's eyes sparkled with fascination. "I wish I could paint like that."

Sean motioned for her to come closer. "You know, anyone can paint. It's about expressing what's in your heart and letting your emotions guide your brush."

The girl looked thoughtful as she considered his words. "I don't know. I've never tried before."

Sean smiled, a sense of connection forming between them. "Would you like to give it a try?"

With a nod, the girl set her backpack down and took a seat in front of an empty canvas. Sean handed her a brush and a palette of colors, guiding her through the process step by step. As she dipped the brush into the paint and began to create, her hesitance transformed into a sense of wonder and delight.

As they painted side by side, Sean shared stories of his own journey—the doubts he had faced, the mistakes he had made, and the faith that had carried him through. The girl listened closely, her own brushstrokes becoming more confident with each passing moment.

When they finally stepped back to admire their creations, a sense of accomplishment filled the room. Sean looked at the girl's painting—a reflection of her own journey of discovery—and then at his own, a reminder of the footprints of faith that had guided him.

"You see," Sean said, his voice gentle, "painting is about more than just colors on a canvas. It's a way to express your heart, to embrace your journey, and to find beauty even in the midst of challenges."

The girl smiled, her eyes shining with newfound understanding. "Thank you, mister. I didn't think I could do it."

Sean's heart swelled with gratitude. "Remember, there's beauty in imperfection. Each brushstroke tells a story, and each painting is a unique reflection of the artist's soul."

As the girl gathered her things to leave, Sean watched her go with a sense of fulfillment. He realized that his own journey of rediscovery had led him to this moment—a moment of connection, inspiration, and the realization that his own footprints of faith had guided him to a place of renewed purpose.

And as he looked at the paintings that beautified the walls of his studio, Sean knew that each stroke of the brush carried with it a piece of his heart— a testament to the journey he had undertaken, the mistakes he had embraced, and the faith that had carried him through the storm.

Sean sat in his studio, his eyes fixed on the paintings that decorated the walls—a gallery of emotions, stories, and moments captured on canvas. The memories of his journey, both inward and outward, seemed to come alive with each stroke of color, each brushstroke that had been carefully applied.

Over time, Sean's art gained attention—local galleries showcased his work, and people were drawn to the honesty and depth that his paintings delivered. His journey of rediscovery had touched a chord within others, serving as a reminder that even in the midst of doubt and uncertainty, there was an opportunity for growth and transformation.

One afternoon, as Sean was arranging his paintings for an upcoming exhibit, his phone buzzed with a notification. He picked it up and read the message— a familiar name appeared on the screen. It was Joi, the friend he had known since childhood.

The message contained an invitation—an invitation to visit her and view her own collection of artwork. Joi had embarked on her own journey of healing and renewal, channeling her experiences and emotions into her art.

With a sense of anticipation, Sean made his way to Joi's studio. As he entered, he was greeted by a display of paintings that reflected a journey of spirit and courage. The room seemed to pulse with a shared understanding— an unspoken bond between two friends who had weathered their own storms.

Joi smiled as she saw Sean, a mixture of gratitude and excitement in her eyes. "I'm so glad you could come, Sean."

Sean looked around the studio, his admiration evident in his expression.

"Your work is incredible, Joi. Each piece tells a story."

Joi's eyes shifted to the painting nearest to her—a canvas decorated with vivid colors and swirling patterns. "This one is my favorite. It's called 'Renewal.' It's about finding strength in vulnerability and embracing the process of healing."

Sean nodded, his eyes lingering on the painting. "It's beautiful, Joi. You've captured the essence of renewal and transformation."

As they talked, Sean and Joi shared their journeys—the challenges they had faced, the doubts they had confronted, and the unexpected ways in which they had found renewal. Their stories echoed one another, a testament to the power of friendship and the courage to embrace the unknown.

As the afternoon turned into evening, Sean and Joi sat by the window, their conversation flowing like the waves outside. They spoke of faith, of the footprints that guided them through life's uncertainties, and of the unbreakable bond they shared.

"You know," Joi said with a smile, "sometimes we have to look back to see how far we've come."

Sean nodded. His heart full. "And sometimes, it's in the midst of challenges that we discover our true strength and purpose."

As Sean looked at Joi's paintings, he realized that their journey had come full circle—a journey of doubt, rediscovery, and renewal. Just as their footprints had left impressions in the sand, their experiences had left imprints on their souls—a testament to their strength and the faith that had carried them through.

And as they sat there, two friends bound by shared experiences and an unwavering friendship, they knew that their footprints of faith would continue to guide them forward—a reminder that even in the face of uncertainty, there was a path illuminated by the light of hope, the colors of resilience, and the brushstrokes of courage.

Part 3: Treasures in the Mundane

CHAPTER 9

Treasures in the Ordinary

The early morning sun cast a warm and gentle glow across the small, attractive town. Susan stood by the window, her fingers tracing the frost patterns that adorned the glass. It was a quiet morning, and as she looked out at the world awakening, she felt a sense of wonder at the beauty that could be found in the most ordinary moments.

"Mornin', sweetheart," Marie's voice chimed as she entered the kitchen, her apron tied around her waist.

Susan turned to her mother, a smile lighting up her face. "Good morning, Mommy. Look at the frost on the window—it's like a painting."

Marie approached Susan; her own eyes fixed on the delicate patterns etched on the glass. "You're right, Susan. Sometimes, it's the simple things that hold the most beauty."

As they shared a quiet moment by the window, a sense of connection passed between mother and daughter—an unspoken understanding of the treasures that could be found in the ordinary.

Later that morning, Susan and Marie decided to take a stroll through the town. The familiar sights—the bustling market, the charming houses, and the friendly faces—filled them with a sense of belonging and community.

As they walked, Marie pointed to an elderly man sitting on a bench, feeding pigeons with a smile on his face. "You know, sometimes it's the small acts of kindness that make a person's day brighter."

Susan nodded, her eyes lingering on the scene. "Like how you make pancakes for breakfast on Sundays."

Marie chuckled; her heart warmed by her daughter's observation. "Exactly, Susan. It's in those moments that we create memories and find joy."

Their journey through the town continued, each step revealing the tapestry of everyday life—the laughter of children playing in the park, the aroma of freshly baked bread fanning from a bakery, and the sound of a musician playing his guitar on a street corner.

As they passed a flower shop, Susan stopped to appreciate a bouquet of lively roses. "Look, Mommy! These flowers are so pretty."

Marie smiled, her eyes reflecting a shared appreciation for life's simple pleasures. "They are, Susan. And you know, just like these flowers, there's beauty in every corner of our lives."

Their stroll led them to a small café nestled in a cozy corner of the town. They settled at a table near the window, the soft hum of conversation and the aroma of coffee filling the air. As they sipped their drinks, Marie shared stories of her own childhood—the memories of growing up in the same town, the friendships that had shaped her, and the lessons she had learned along the way.

"Life is full of surprises, Susan," Marie said with a smile. "Sometimes, the most ordinary moments turn out to be the ones we cherish the most."

Susan looked out the window, her gaze fixed on the bystanders. "I want to remember all these moments, Mommy—the frost on the window, the flowers, the people."

Marie reached across the table and placed her hand on Susan's. "You know, sweetheart, you have a gift for finding the extraordinary in the ordinary. It's a quality that will serve you well in life."

As they left the café and continued their walk, Susan's heart felt full—a sense of gratitude for the moments they had shared, the stories they had exchanged, and the bond they had deepened.

When they returned home, Marie and Susan stood by the window once more, their hands pressed against the glass. The sun had risen higher in the sky, casting a warm light over the town. Marie's heart swelled with a sense of contentment—a realization that the treasures in life were not always found in grand gestures, but in the quiet moments of connection, love, and appreciation.

"Thank you, Mommy," Susan said softly, her eyes fixed on the world outside.

Marie smiled; her heart touched by her daughter's gratitude. "No, Susan, thank you. Thank you for reminding me to find beauty in the everyday—to treasure the simple moments that make life truly extraordinary."

As this mother and daughter stood by the window, holding on to the present—a treasure in itself—knowing that the journey of life was laced with the threads of ordinary moments, cherished memories, and a love that exceeded the ordinary.

CHAPTER 10

When Hearts Align

The church bells echoed through the crisp morning air as Michelle and Valerie made their way to the small, charming House of Worship that had become a place of relief and connection for them. The sun's golden rays filtered through the stained-glass windows, casting colorful patterns on the wooden pews and the stone floors.

As they took their seats, Michelle's eyed swept over the church—the place where she had found comfort, guidance, and a sense of belonging. Valerie sat beside her, her small hand slipping into Michelle's, a gesture of unity and love.

The familiar hymn filled the church as the congregation joined in song, their voices blending in harmony all while singing, Blessed Assurance. Michelle closed her eyes, her heart lifting with the melody—a reminder that even during life's challenges, there was a sense of beauty and connection that transcended the ordinary.

After the service, Michelle and Valerie lingered for a moment, their eyes fixed on the altar—a symbol of faith, hope, and the mysteries of the divine. As they stood in the presence of the sacred space, a sense of peace enveloped them—a reminder that their journey was guided by a force greater than themselves.

"Mommy," Valerie whispered, her voice soft as a gentle breeze, "do you think our hearts are like puzzle pieces that fit together?"

Michelle looked down at her daughter, her heart touched by the innocence and wisdom in her words. "Yes, Valerie. I believe that sometimes, when hearts align, they create something beautiful—a bond that can weather any storm."

Valerie's gaze remained fixed on the altar, her thoughts a canvas of curiosity and contemplation. "Just like the stained-glass windows. They're made of different pieces, but when the sunlight shines through, they create something magical."

Michelle knelt beside Valerie; their hands still locked together—a physical example of the connection they shared. "You have a way of seeing the world through a beautiful lens, Valerie."

As they left the chapel, Michelle and Valerie walked along a path that led to a small garden. The air was filled with the fragrance of thriving flowers, and the sound of birdsong seemed to entertain their steps.

"Mommy," Valerie said, her eyes turning to the flowers, "do you think each flower has its own story?"

Michelle smiled, her heart touched by her daughter's perception. "I believe so. Just like people, each flower has its own journey—its own struggles and triumphs."

They continued their walk, Michelle and Valerie sharing stories and dreams—the threads that laced their lives together into a place of connection. As they talked, Michelle's thoughts turned to William—a man whose presence in her life had brought a new chapter of hope and companionship.

" Valerie," Michelle began, her voice gentle, "there's someone I want you to meet."

Valerie looked at her mother with curiosity, her eyes shining. "Who is it, Mommy?"

Michelle's eyes drifted to a bench placed among the flowers—a bench where William sat, his eyes fixed on a book in his hands. Michelle's heart skipped a beat as she took a step forward, Valerie following closely behind.

"Hi, William," Michelle said with a smile, her voice carrying a mixture of warmth and anticipation.

William looked up, his eyes meeting Michelle's with a hint of surprise.

"Michelle, Valerie —what a wonderful surprise."

Michelle introduced William to Valerie, their eyes locking in a moment of shared recognition—a recognition of the connection that had deepened between them over time. As they talked, Michelle felt a sense of comfort and ease—a reminder that when hearts aligned, conversations flowed effortlessly.

" Valerie was just telling me about the stained-glass windows and the flowers," Michelle said, her eyes shifting to William.

William smiled, his eyes crinkling at the corners. "It sounds like Valerie has a knack for finding beauty in the world around her."

Valerie nodded, her eyes moving between Michelle and William. "Mommy says that sometimes, when hearts align, they create something beautiful."

Michelle's heart swelled with pride as she looked at her daughter—a testament to the wisdom that came from her young heart.

" Valerie is right," William said softly, his voice a melody of understanding. "When hearts align, they create a bond that can withstand anything."

As the three of them sat on the bench, surrounded by the beauty of the garden, Michelle felt a sense of gratitude—a gratitude for the journey that had brought them to this moment, for the connections that had formed, and for the hope that had blossomed unexpectedly.

And as the sun dipped below the horizon, casting a warm, golden glow over the garden, Michelle, Valerie, and William shared a moment of unity—a moment that captured the essence of their shared journey, their aligned hearts, and the promise of a future displaying a connection, love, and the beauty found in the simplest of moments.

CHAPTER 11

The Power of Presence

The rain fell in a soft, rhythmic pattern, casting a serene atmosphere over the town. Paul stood by the window of his art studio; his eyes fixed on the drops that danced on the glass—a reflection of the emotions that spun around within him.

The past few months had been a whirlwind—a mix of creative highs and personal challenges. Paul's art had gained recognition, and his pieces were being featured in galleries beyond the town's borders. Yet, among the success, he had felt a growing sense of isolation—an ache for companionship and understanding.

One evening, as the rain continued to fall, Paul's phone buzzed with a message—a message from Brooke, a friend he had met during a time of rediscovery. The message contained an invitation—an invitation to a gathering at her home.

With a mixture of curiosity and anticipation, Paul made his way to Brooke's house. As he entered, he was greeted by a warm, inviting atmosphere—the soft glow of candles, the aroma of home-cooked food, and the sound of laughter echoing through the rooms.

"Brooke," Paul said with a smile, "thank you for inviting me."

Brooke smiled in return, her eyes holding a mixture of welcome and understanding. "We're glad you could make it, Paul."

As the evening unfolded, Paul found himself engaged in conversations with familiar faces—the people he had met during his journey in the town. The warmth of their interactions brought a sense of belonging—an affirmation that even during challenges, connections could be nurtured.

Later in the evening, as the rain continued to fall outside, the group gathered in the living room. Brooke's daughter, Jewel, sat on the floor, her eyes bright with curiosity as she listened to the stories being shared.

"Paul," Brooke said, her voice carrying a gentle invitation, "would you share one of your paintings with us? We'd love to see your work."

Paul hesitated for a moment, his emotions spinning within him. But as he looked around the room—the faces of people who had become his friends, his companions on the journey—he felt a sense of trust and vulnerability.

He retrieved a painting from his bag—a piece that expressed his journey of rediscovery, his challenges, and his moments of inspiration. As he held the painting, he began to speak, his voice carrying the weight of his experiences. "This painting," Paul began, his eyes fixed on the canvas, "represents a journey—a journey of doubt, of rediscovery, and of the power of connection. Each brushstroke tells a story—a story of the emotions that I've wrestled with, the doubts I've faced, and the hope that has emerged."

As Paul spoke, the room fell into a hush—a testament to the power of vulnerability, the beauty of shared stories, and the magic that could unfold when hearts opened to one another.

When he finished speaking, Brooke reached out and placed a hand on Paul's shoulder—a gesture of understanding and support. "Thank you for sharing that, Paul. Your painting reflects your journey, and we're grateful that you chose to share it with us."

Paul looked around the room, his eyes meeting the eyes of those who had gathered. In their presence, he felt a sense of connection—a reminder that the power of vulnerability and presence could bridge the gaps that life's challenges sometimes created.

As the evening ended, Paul realized that he had found a circle of friends—people who had walked alongside him during his journey, who had shared their own stories, and who had reminded him of the strength that could be found in unity.

"You know," Brooke said, her voice carrying a depth of emotion,

"Sometimes, the greatest gift we can offer is our presence—the simple act of showing up and being there for one another."

Paul nodded in agreement; his heart filled with gratitude. "You're right, Brooke. The power of presence is a gift that can heal, inspire, and strengthen us on our journeys."

And as the rain continued to fall outside, the group shared a moment of unity—a moment that captured the essence of their shared experiences, their openness, and the realization that in the company of friends, the power of presence could lighten even the darkest of moments.

CHAPTER 12

Small Acts, Big Impact

The town was buzzing with excitement as preparations for the annual community fair were in full swing. Decorative banners fluttered in the breeze, and colorful booths were being set up along the streets— anticipation and unity was in the air.

Among the lively crowd was Julie, her eyes wide with wonder as she took in the sights and sounds around her. Amanda walked beside her, a smile on her face as she watched her daughter's excitement.

"Mommy, look at all the stalls!" Julie shouted; her voice filled with delight.

Amanda chuckled; her heart warmed by Julie's excitement. "There's so much to see, isn't there?"

As they wandered through the fair, Amanda and Julie came across a booth decorated with handwritten signs and a banner that read "Random Acts of Kindness." A group of volunteers stood by, inviting bystanders to participate.

Julie tugged on Amanda's sleeve, her eyes shining. "Mommy, can we do a random act of kindness?"

Amanda's heart swelled with pride at her daughter's request. "Of course, Julie. What do you have in mind?"

Julie scanned the booth and spotted a stack of colorful cards. Each card contained a simple act of kindness that could be carried out throughout the fair. Julie picked one up and read it aloud, her voice eager.

"Give someone a genuine compliment."

Amanda smiled, her heart touched by the simplicity and power of the act.

"That's a wonderful idea, Julie."

They walked through the fair, their eyes fixed on the people around them—strangers who were part of the same community, each with their own stories and experiences.

As they approached a woman selling handcrafted jewelry, Julie's eyes landed on a bracelet decorated with beads. She turned to Amanda with a determined expression.

"Mommy, I want to give her a compliment," Julie said, with a firm voice.

Amanda nodded, her heart swelling with pride. "Go ahead, Julie. I'm right here with you."

Julie took a deep breath and walked up to the woman. "Excuse me," she said with a smile, "your jewelry is really pretty. I like all the colors."

The woman looked at Julie, her eyes softening with warmth. "Thank you, sweetheart. I appreciate your kind words."

As Amanda and Julie walked away, Amanda felt a sense of awe at her daughter's ability to connect and brighten someone's day with a simple compliment.

"Julie," Amanda said as they continued their walk, "that was a beautiful thing you did."

Julie's smile radiated with joy. "I just wanted her to know that her work is special."

Amanda's heart swelled with love for her daughter—the example of the small acts of kindness that could create ripples of positivity in the world.

Later in the day, Amanda and Julie came across a booth where children were crafting colorful friendship bracelets. Julie's eyes lit up, and she eagerly joined in, her fingers neatly weaving the threads together.

As they worked, Amanda struck up a conversation with the booth volunteers—a group of teenagers who were raising funds for a local charity. Amanda learned about their dedication to making a difference and their commitment to supporting those in need.

"Mommy," Julie said as she finished crafting a bracelet, "can we give this bracelet to the kind lady we met earlier?"

Amanda nodded; her heart touched by Julie's thoughtfulness. "That's a wonderful idea, Julie. I'm sure she'll appreciate it."

They made their way back to the jewelry booth, where the woman was arranging her pieces. Julie approached her; her eyes filled with excitement.

"We made this bracelet for you," Julie said, extending the laced creation toward the woman.

Tears sparkled in the woman's eyes as she accepted the bracelet. "Thank you, sweetheart. This means so much to me."

As they walked away, Amanda and Julie shared a moment of connection—a moment that embodied the spirit of the fair and the impact of small acts of kindness.

"Julie," Amanda said softly, "you have a gift for making people feel special."

Julie smiled; her heart filled with contentment. "I just want everyone to know that they matter."

And as the sun began to set, casting a warm, glow over the fair, Amanda and Julie continued their journey—two souls who had embraced the power of small acts, recognizing that even the tiniest gestures of kindness could have a profound impact on the lives they touched.

CHAPTER 13

Intertwined in Love

The town was glowing with the warm twilight as Morgan and Douglas found themselves at the heart of a special event—a community gathering that celebrated unity, connection, and the bonds that had been forged over time.

Colorful lamps swung gently in the breeze, casting a soft and inviting light over the crowd. Laughter and conversation filled the air, creating a sense of company that seemed to exceed time and place.

Morgan stood by the lamp-lit path, a feeling of gratitude welling up within her. The journey she had started brought her to this moment—an evening of togetherness and celebration.

As the crowd mingled, Morgan's eyes found Douglas, who stood a short distance away. His eyes met hers, and a smile played at the corners of his lips—a smile that carried understanding and companionship.

Douglas approached Morgan, his eyes reflecting the warmth of the lamps. "Beautiful evening, isn't it?"

Morgan nodded, her heart ringing the emotion. "It truly is, Douglas. It's amazing to see how the threads of our lives have merged themselves together."

Douglas's fingers brushed against the lamps as they passed, the gentle paper and soft light symbolizing the tender and beauty of the connections that had been formed.

"You know," Douglas said, his voice a mixture of thought and emotion, "sometimes it's the moments like these—the ones filled with laughter, friendship, and love—that remind us of what truly matters."

Morgan's eyes stayed on the lamps, the scene a visual representation of the linking threads that had shaped her journey. "It's the people we meet, the connections we form, and the memories we create that link us."

As the evening unfolded, Morgan and Douglas found themselves deep in conversations with friends old and new. The stories shared were a testament to the diversity and depth of experiences that had brought the community together.

Nearby, Lindsey was engaged in a lively conversation with a group of children. Her laughter carried on the breeze, a reminder of the innocence and joy that illuminated the present moment.

Morgan turned to Douglas; her voice soft yet steadfast. "You've been a part of this journey, Douglas —a part that laced our lives together."

Douglas's eyes held a depth of emotion as he looked at Morgan. "And you've been a guiding light—a reminder that even in the face of challenges, there's a path brightened by faith, connection, and love."

The night sky above them began to sparkle with stars, each one a reminder of the vastness of the universe and the connection of all living beings.

"I never imagined that a journey of rediscovery would lead to such depth of connection," Morgan said, her voice carrying a mixture of wonder and gratitude.

Douglas nodded, his heart resonating with her words. "Sometimes, it's in the unexpected moments that we find the greatest treasures—moments tied in love and shared experiences."

As the evening wore on, Morgan and Douglas found themselves by the lamp-lit path once more—a path that seemed to stretch into the infinite horizon, much like the future that lay ahead.

" Douglas," Morgan began, her voice steady, "you've been a part of this journey—a journey that has unfolded with its own twists and turns, its own challenges and triumphs."

Douglas looked at Morgan, his eyes unwavering. "And you, Morgan, have been the thread that's held it all together—a thread of strength, grace, and unwavering faith."

Morgan reached out and took Douglas's hand—a gesture of connection that felt both natural and profound. As they stood there, surrounded by the lamps' gentle glow, they felt a sense of unity—a unity that was built on shared experiences, mutual respect, and the unspoken understanding of the journey they had walked.

And as the lamps continued to swing in the evening breeze, Morgan and Douglas embraced the present—a present linked in love—a testament to the connections that had been formed, the bonds that had been deepened, and the promise of a future brightened by the light of unity and companionship.

CHAPTER 14

Beyond the Surface

The sun hung low in the sky, casting a warm and gentle light over the town. Yvonne stood by the calm lake, her reflection mirrored on the surface of the water—a reminder of the journey she had started, the connections she had formed, and the depths that lay beyond the surface.

The past year had been a whirlwind of experiences—simply put, a thread of faith, friendship, and the unexpected turns that life often took. As she stood by the water's edge, Yvonne found herself lost in thought—a reflection on the chapters that had unfolded and the lessons that had been learned.

Footsteps approached from behind, and Yvonne turned to see Brian approaching—the man whose presence had become a steady anchor in her life.

"Beautiful day, isn't it?" Brian said, his voice carrying a touch of longing.

Yvonne nodded; her eyes relaxed on the ripples that danced on the lake's surface. "It's a day for reflection—a day to look beyond the surface and contemplate the journey."

Brian walked beside Yvonne; his eyes fixed on the horizon. "Sometimes, the most meaningful experiences lie beneath the surface—the stories that aren't always visible but shape who we are."

Yvonne's heart resonated with his words, a testament to the shared understanding that had grown between them. "You're right, Brian. It's the moments of vulnerability, the connections formed, and the emotions felt that shape the narrative of our lives."

As they walked along the lake's edge, Yvonne, and Brian shared stories—the chapters of their pasts that had brought them to this moment. Their conversations were a testament to the beauty of transparency—the willingness to open and share the layers of their experiences.

" Brian," Yvonne began, her voice a mixture of curiosity and emotion, "what inspired you to become an artist?"

Brian's eyes shone with memories as he looked at Yvonne. "Art has always been a way for me to express what words couldn't express. It's a canvas for my emotions, my thoughts, and the stories that I carry within."

Yvonne's eyes turned to the water, her reflection a reminder of the layers that made up her own story. "And what about you, Yvonne? What inspired you to begin on this journey?"

Yvonne took a deep breath, her gaze never leaving the water. "It was a journey of rediscovery—a journey to reclaim my faith, my sense of purpose, and my connection with God and the world around me. The town, the people I've met, and the connections I've formed—they've all been instrumental in guiding me back to my true self."

Brian nodded, a sense of understanding passing between them. "It's in the moments of self-discovery that we often find the most profound connections with others."

As the sun began to dip below the horizon, casting a warm, orange glow over the water, Yvonne and Brian shared a moment of unity—a moment that captured the essence of their journey, their shared understanding, and the promise of the future.

" Brian," Yvonne said softly, "thank you for being a part of my journey—for walking beside me, for sharing your stories, and for reminding me that there's beauty beyond the surface."

Brian's fingers brushed against Yvonne's, the touch sending a shiver of connection through them. " Yvonne, you've brought depth and meaning to my life—a depth that goes beyond what's visible on the surface."

As they stood by the lake, surrounded by the beauty of the world around them, Yvonne and Brian embraced the present—a present that held the power of vulnerability, the beauty of shared experiences, and the promise of a future where the layers of connection continued to weave their stories together.

CHAPTER 15

Echoes of Eternity

The sun began to fade, casting a warm, golden light over the town—an echo of the beauty that had unfolded throughout Kirsten's journey. The air was filled with a sense of anticipation as the townspeople gathered in the heart of the town—a gathering that marked a peak of connections, growth, and the echoes of eternity that resonated through each chapter.

Kirsten stood before a podium; her heart filled with gratitude for the journey that had led her to this moment. Beside her stood Ray, his presence alone was the reassuring anchor Kirsten needed.

As she looked out at the faces before her—friends, associates, and the people who had walked alongside her— Kirsten's voice carried with emotion. "Thank you all for being here," Kirsten began, her voice steady yet filled with the depth of her experiences. "This journey has shared its moments— moments of growth, of connection, and of the echoes of life that bind us."

The crowd listened intently, the atmosphere charged with anticipation and the weight of shared experiences.

Kirsten's eyes turned to Ray, their eyes meeting—a silent exchange that delivered a depth of their connection. "And there's someone here who has been a very important part of this journey—a companion who has walked beside me, shared his stories, and reminded me of the beauty that lies in the everyday."

She turned back to the crowd, her voice firm. "Ray, would you please join me?"

Ray stepped forward; his eyes fixed on Kirsten. As they stood side by side, Kirsten continued, with the emotion and certainty in her voice. "Ray, your presence has been a reminder that connections are tied beyond the surface— that the threads of our lives are meant to intersect in the most unexpected and beautiful ways."

Kirsten extended her hand to Ray, a gesture of unity and appreciation. "In recognition of our journey—of the shared experiences, the growth, and the echoes of eternity that have shaped us—I'd like to present you with this plague."

Ray's fingers brushed against the plague, his eyes reflecting a mixture of gratitude and emotion. " Kirsten, this means more than words can express. It's a symbol of the threads that have united our stories together—a reminder of the journey we've walked and the connections we've formed."

The crowd watched in silence, a tangible sense of unity and connection enveloping them.

Kirsten handed the plague to Ray, their eyes locking in a moment of shared understanding—a recognition of the depth of their bond.

"Thank you," Ray said softly, "for being a part of my journey—for reminding me that there's beauty in vulnerability, strength in connection, and understanding moments that shape our lives."

Kirsten smiled, her heart brimming with appreciation. "Thank you, Ray, for reminding me of the echoes of eternity—the threads of connection that resonate far beyond the confines of time."

As the sun dipped below the horizon, casting a warm and radiant glow over the gathering, the crowd exploded into applause—a chorus of appreciation for the journey that had been shared, the connections that had been formed, and the beauty that had been tied their lives.

Kirsten and Ray stood before the crowd, their eyes reflecting the journey they had started —a journey that had led them to this moment of unity, connection, and the echoes of eternity that whispered through the chapters of their lives.

ACKNOWLEDGMENTS

Writing a novel is a journey that would not be possible without the support, inspiration, and encouragement of numerous individuals who contribute their time, insights, and unwavering belief in the power of storytelling. As the author of "Miracles in Ordinary Moments," I am deeply grateful to those who have played a role in bringing this story to life.

To my family, who have been my pillars of strength and my biggest cheerleaders—I am indebted to your love, understanding, and endless support. Your belief in me has been a guiding light on this journey.

To my friends, who have provided me with laughter, companionship, and the necessary breaks to recharge—I appreciate your presence more than words can express.

To my readers, who embark on this journey with open hearts and open minds—I am humbled by your willingness to explore the world of this novel. Your engagement and curiosity are the driving force behind my words.

To the characters of this story, who have taken on lives of their own and allowed me to explore the depths of human emotions and connections—thank you for guiding me through the twists and turns of the narrative.

To the editors, designers, and publishing team who have dedicated their expertise to bringing this book to fruition—your commitment to excellence is evident on every page.

And finally, I extend my heartfelt thanks, love and appreciation to my wife, Katrina, whose unwavering support and encouragement made this journey of writing fun and pure bliss of happiness."

With Gratitude,

Lionel B. Pearson

To God Be the Glory of the Great Things He Has Done!!!

www.ingramcontent.com/pod-product-compliance
Lightning Source LLC
LaVergne TN
LVHW041458070426
835507LV00009B/673